WISDOM AND COMMON SENSE
FOR THE YOUNG MAN

God Bless You

Ray Wilson

Ray Wilson, DD

WISDOM AND COMMON SENSE FOR THE YOUNG MAN
by Ray Wilson, DD

Printed in the United States of America

ISBN 978-1-60266-770-9

www.xulonpress.com

THANKS

Special thanks to Rose Belcher who faithfully spent many hours correcting my grammar and spelling.

Rose is a retired school teacher and administrator, with a BSinEd, MAinEd, and an MCEADMIN. She has authored books and is a very special person.

Also thank you to my wife who encouraged me to write this book. Also to Daddy Wise, who introduced me to the book of Proverbs.

Also to the Pastors, Sunday School teachers and many others to numerous to mention.

DEDICATION

—∞∞∞—

This book is dedicated to Daddy Wise, who taught me to study and memorize the Proverbs. Also to our son Ray Jr., our 10 grandsons, and five great grandsons. I pray they will live, walk, and talk with wisdom and common sense. And I would not leave out my wonderful wife who encouraged me by her example of what a wife should be. She helped teach Wisdom to our four children who are all in Pastoral ministry. And of our 20 grandchildren, the six oldest are in full time ministry and the next graduates from Bible College this year and then another will attend Bible College next semester. We are just eager to see our fourteen great grandchildren serving the Lord in some capacity.

And to the wonderful young men I have had the pleasure to share my life with during my 57 years of ministry. I dedicate this work.

To the young men I had the privilege of having a part in their life when I pastored, watching them grow up and become men of honesty, integrity and wisdom.

Also to the many young men we had attending the many camp programs through the years.

And last but not least, the many men we have been able to help through our men's homes of restoration. I pray they will gain Godly wisdom while in the restoration program.

PREAMBLE

⸺ ∞ ⸺

With changes in society, and moral guidelines a thing of the past, our young people need some kind of guidance today.

First let me say, "your conscience is always a good guide." Conscience will always tell you to do right, it will always lead you in the right way. So do not listen to other voices; let your conscience be your guide.

Conscience and common sense go together. Adam and Eve's conscience told them they had done wrong. No book was written, just something that was put in them when they were created, their conscience.

In this book, we add "Wisdom" to common sense. Learn "Wisdom and Common Sense." Think on the many words of wisdom, memorize these words from the wisest man who ever lived, learn from him.

When you put wisdom and common sense with your conscience, you will not go wrong.

Happy reading....

FORWARD

—ⒸⒸⒸ—

After WW2, I spent some time with an older and respected man named Mr. Wise. He was a well known minister in Southern California. He preached often on prophecy and I wanted to have him teach me the book of Daniel.

He willingly did this, but was constantly telling me to read the Proverbs because it was written to the young man, also to memorize the Proverbs. He would say, "these contain wisdom for your daily life."

I did this and from that time my regular morning prayer has been, "Lord give me wisdom for today."

Recently while reading the Proverbs again, I felt it would be difficult to get young men to read the Proverbs today. It is not easy to understand and seems jumbled to the young people.

I felt if it was in today's language it would be received better.

So I have taken **WORDS OF WISDOM BY THE WISEST MAN WHO EVER LIVED** and rewritten them in the language of today then put them together in categories.

This book is the result of that. I pray that many young men will have a desire to gain wisdom and common sense. And this book will help in their search for all that God has for them.

INDEX

WORDS OF WISDOM FOR YOUNG MEN

———⚭———

This book is written to show young men how to live and what to do in every circumstance- to be understanding, fair and just in everything you do.

Every young man who obeys these instructions will receive wisdom and common sense. Search through these treasures of wisdom and you will receive better insight and discernment. Then wisdom will be natural.

It is the desire of the author of these words to make the simple-minded wise and to warn about problems you will face in life. If you pay attention to these words, the wise will become wiser and become leaders by learning and applying these truths.

How can you become wise? Just as in learning to walk, the first step is to trust and reverence God.

A fool refuses wisdom and does not want to be taught. Learn these words of wisdom, apply them to your life and many men will honor you.

God gives wisdom. In His Word is knowledge and understanding. To those who love and respect Him, He gives good common sense. He shows how to tell right from wrong and how to make right decisions.

Your heart and mind will be filled with wisdom and your life will be full of joy.

Some young men think only evil thoughts and want you to be a partner in their crimes; robbing, stealing and killing their victims.

Young man, never forget what is taught in these words of wisdom. To live a long and satisfying life, follow the instruction wisdom gives. Always be kind and truthful, hold these things as valuable to you. Write them in your mind.

If you want favor with man, a good reputation, be known to have good judgment and common sense. Then put your complete trust in God and His word. Put God first in your life, He will never direct you to do wrong and will bring success to your life.

Wisdom gives a long, good life, full of honor, pleasure, peace and riches.

The young man who uses good judgment and common sense, who knows right from wrong, is a happy person. What he has in life is more valuable than great riches.

Wisdom will tell you to stay away from people who will take you the wrong way. there are some young men who will say, "come with us, we will show you excitement." but what they do is against God's law and man's law.

Nothing can compare to wisdom from God. Your life will be like a tree planted by the rivers of water, good fruit grows on it. So, eat the fruit of this tree and you will be happy. Keep on eating it.

Have two main goals in your life. Wisdom should be number one and common sense number two. These will teach you to do what is right, so don't lose these two. Wisdom and common sense will keep you safe from the problems of life that lead to defeat and disaster.

People will trust you when you use wisdom and common sense. Value their trust, build on it and work at it.

Learn this truth. When you live a life of doing what is right, this is the wisest life you can live. If you live a right life, carrying out the instructions of wisdom and common sense, they will lead you to an exciting life, real living.

Let me say this again, I cannot over emphasize this. Learn to be wise, develop good judgment and common sense. Live a life doing what you know is right, follow the instruction of wisdom, it will lead you to an exciting life.

Let wisdom tell you to avoid evil people. They do not rest until they cause someone to fail. They are full of lies and deceit. But the man who does what is right, knowing he is walking in the light of his understanding of wisdom, is like a bright new day.

You probably have heard someone say, "he is worthless". Let me explain to you a worthless, wicked person. He lies all the time, rebels at anything good and worthwhile. He causes trouble between people, thinks constantly about doing evil, sneaky things. Problems and trouble will come upon him and he will have no help.

WHAT GOD DOES NOT LIKE

- A person who is proud
- One who lies
- A murderer
- A person who plans to do wrong
- One who tells lies about another person
- A person who causes problems between people

When these words penetrate your mind, they are a light in a dark place, to warn you of danger and lead you to do right.

Listen to the voice of wisdom and common sense. Look for wisdom and you will find it. Wisdom is everywhere, it is not hidden. Wisdom and understanding are available to everyone, they are free.

Wisdom will give you important information to guide your life. Wisdom is always right and true. Wisdom is plain and simple to a person with an open mind.

Value wisdom above anything else. Wisdom and knowledge come together and cause you to have good judgment.

Fear, love and respect God and you will hate evil, it will bring a distaste to your mouth. Wisdom hates evil, pride, lovers of self, deceit and corrupt minds.

Because of wisdom and common sense, rulers lead their people, judges make right decisions, and wisdom gives understanding and power

The way of wisdom is justice and right. Those who look for wisdom will find it. Wisdom has been available to people all the time.

Wisdom was created before God formed the earth and heavens. Wisdom was shown in all creation. Wisdom was always with God and is a part of God and God gives this wisdom to us freely. You cannot buy wisdom, you must seek it. Search all parts of your life for wisdom and you will find it.

Wisdom is the greatest treasure you will have. Follow wisdom and you will have a happy life.

WISDOM SAYS,
"COME LOOK AND LEARN"

———— ∞∞∞ ————

L earn to love, fear and honor God. For this is the begin-
ning of wisdom. Understanding comes from knowing
God.

Wisdom and common sense will make all your efforts
more profitable. Therefore, your life will be more fruitful,
because wisdom will help you.

Riches taken by doing wrong is not good and you will
live with guilt. But doing right and good brings joy and
happiness.

Use wisdom and common sense and you will accept
instruction. If you think you know it all, you will fail.

A good man's feet will follow the paths of light shown
by the Word of God. A person who tries to go another way
will be lost.

Committing even a little sin will bring guilt and sorrow.
Discipline from God's Word gives peace and Joy

Hatred causes bitterness and can stir up quarrels or fights. But compassion will overlook even insults

Young men who use common sense are often sought out as counselors. Store up learning while you are young.

Hold your tongue while in conversations. Do not blurt out what you know. Use wisdom and common sense.

Listen to good teaching, it will take you to the path of God. A person who will not listen will lose the way.

It is better to have a listening ear; you will learn much. But a person who talks too much will soon put his foot in his mouth. Be wise and careful with what you say. Learn to shut your mouth

When a good man speaks, listen to him. When a Godly man gives advice, pay attention. This advice can make you rich.

It is fun to use wisdom and common sense. When you want what is right, you will find it.

Wisdom and common sense is like an anchor in a storm. A fool is blown away and destroyed with it. But wisdom will hold a young man to truth.

God's ways provide a strong foundation and when trouble comes you will not be shaken.

The mind of one who is right with God shows wisdom, and what he speaks will be pleasing to others.

A person who uses wisdom and common sense is guided by his honesty. The Lord hates cheating, and the evil man is destroyed by his dishonesty

Evil words of jealousy and gossip will destroy, but wisdom from God rebuilds.

The influence of Godly people who use wisdom and common sense will cause a city to prosper. But moral decay will cause a city to become a slum area.

Without wisdom among leaders, a nation is headed for problems. But in those who rely on wisdom and common sense is good counsel.

Your spirit is lifted up when you are kind. The good man will have a good life.

If you seek and look for good, you will find God's blessings.

A wise and Godly man is like a tree that bears fruit, and the man who wins souls to God is wise.

If you want to learn, you must be willing and desire to be taught.

A man who uses good common sense is admired; he thinks on honest thoughts.

If you tell the truth, you will find satisfaction in life.

You will be known by your truthfulness, because truth will stand the test of time.

God delights in honesty and those who keep their promises.

Control your tongue, you may win an argument by careful conversation. A quick retort can ruin all your plans.

Hate lies and your life will be full of light. Your goodness will help give you direction for your life.

It is true that some people who are very rich are really very poor. While there are those who are poor in this world's goods, yet, they are very rich.

Young man, listen and be very humble. Take advice and become wise. Do not refuse to listen to criticism or you will find yourself in trouble. Accept criticism and you are on your way to victory.

Common sense says if you despise God's word, you will be in trouble. Obey God's word and see exciting results in your life.

FIND A WISE PERSON

Listen to the wise person. His wisdom is like a cool drink of water on a hot day. His wisdom will keep you from problems that are ahead of you.

A wise person thinks and plans ahead. It is exciting to see your plans develop.

Find wise men, make their acquaintance, keep company with them, listen and become wise.

When you do right, you honor God; when you sin, you dishonor God.

Stay away from a foolish person; his advice will be misleading.

A person who is easy to fool believes everything he is told. But a wise man checks what he hears.

One who has a quick temper is a foolish person. A wise man is cautious and avoids anger.

Reverence for the Lord is like a fountain of life. Its waters give long life.

A heart that has peace gives life to the body. But wrong desires rot life.

RESPECT FOR THE POOR

A person who makes life hard for the poor is an insult to God. When you help the poor, you honor God.

Wisdom is in the heart of the man who uses common sense.

Being right with God makes a great nation, but sin brings shame to any people.

A calm answer turns away anger, but harsh words stir up anger.

A teacher who uses wisdom and common sense has students who enjoy learning. A rebellious teacher talks foolishness.

Constant complaining causes problems, but speaking words of life and encouragement brings happiness.

The eyes of the Lord are like a surveillance camera, recording both good and bad.

The Lord loves the young man who does what is right and good. But He hates the sin that causes a young man to turn away from God.

A happy heart brings joy, a sad heart brings sorrow.

CONTROL YOUR THOUGHTS

⎯⎯∽∾∾⎯⎯

A young man is wise who is searching for the truth.

When a young man is happy, everything is good and joyful; but sadness causes things to go wrong.

A young man with a quick temper causes fights and trouble. But a cool head brings peace and quiet.

When you plan your life, seek advice; there is wisdom in many counselors.

When asked, give good sound advice; you will enjoy this. Watch what you say and you will say what is right for the time.

My son, use common sense. Think about what you are going to say, before you speak.

Follow God and His Word, and your life will be like the upward marks on a graph.

Wisdom says, look on things that are good and only listen to good things. These give happiness and health.

Listen and learn from constructive criticism and you will become a wise man.

WISDOM TEACHES

W isdom teaches you to fear the Lord, and exercising humility shows wisdom.

A man makes plans for his life, but only God knows what is going to happen.

You can always prove you are right in your own eyes, but what does God think?

The Lord and people look with disgust on the proud person.

Serve and reverence God, avoid evil things and thoughts.

When your life is pleasing to God, He will make your enemies to be at peace with you.

Pride can destroy your life; a proud spirit causes you to fail.

You will be happy when you put your trust in the Lord. Learn to live according to God's Word and you will be blessed.

Always talk and respond in a pleasant way and people will listen and learn. A wise person uses common sense while speaking.

Wisdom is like an artesian well giving life to those who use it. A person teaches by the way he acts. Kind words are like honey, sweet and easy to accept.

Idle hands and thoughts give the devil opportunity to persuade you to do wrong. Idle lips cause problems. Gossip will cause you to lose friends

Wisdom teaches us to be slow to anger and that self control is better than to be a famous leader.

The joy of a grandparent is in the grandchildren, and a son's pride and joy is in a Godly father.

A man with common sense accepts rebuke and learns from it.

To argue with a person is like a storm. It begins with a little rain and becomes a flood, ruining everything in its path. So don't let an argument begin.

A glad and happy heart is like good tasting medicine. But a sad heart is contagious to all people around it.

To have wisdom is the aim of the understanding young man. But the eyes of a fool are always looking for something for nothing.

He who uses common sense is careful in what he says. Understanding brings a calm spirit.

Listen to the words of a wise man. They are like an artisan well, giving wisdom in an endless supply of water that brings life to all who drink it.

A wise man is open to new ideas, he will look for them.

A man who can give wise advice satisfies the spirit like a good meal to a hungry person.

Some people talk too much and bring trouble for themselves. A wise man listens and gets others to talk.

If you want to have friends you must be friendly. There is a friend that stays closer than a brother.

A rebellious person does not care about understanding or facts, but is only concerned about getting his own way.

A person that separates himself from others and God, only cares about himself and refuses to listen to wisdom and common sense.

If you give a false witness or lie, you will not go unpunished, and you will not get away with it.

Search for wisdom and common sense. Seek understanding and you will prosper and find a good life.

Wisdom and common sense tells us to be slow to anger and overlook insults.

Keep God's Word in your heart and mind; live it and you will live. Turn from God's Word and you will die.

Show kindness and give to the poor and God will bless and repay you.

Listen to counsel, receive instruction and correction, then share the wisdom with others.

You may have many plans for your life, but seek God's wisdom and purpose for your life, His plan will be best.

Loyalty, kindness, integrity and honesty are what people look for in a person they want to work or live with.

SEARCH FOR TRUTH

L ove, worship, and respect for the Lord will bring a good life of joy and happiness.

Do not listen to those who will teach you to ignore what wisdom and common sense tells you is right.

Wine and hard liquor bring false courage and lead to fights. A man is a fool who lets liquor be his master. Anyone can recognize a drunk as he staggers down the street.

It is an honor to walk away from a fight. Only a foolish person will stand and fight.

Many will brag about their loyalty and friendship to you. Search for truth in the way they act.

A Godly person lives a life of integrity. His family is blessed.

God is displeased with any kind of cheating.

You will be known by your actions, whether what you do is good, pure, and right.

God gave you ears to hear, eyes to see and common sense to show you what is right.

The Lord hates all cheating and dishonesty.

Do not try to get even with the person who has done something wrong to you. Let the Lord handle the problem.

A young man's direction in life is ordered by the Lord. Why question? Try to understand His leading.

It is not wise to make a promise to God without considering the cost.

Your conscience is like a voice from God. It reveals to you God's direction for your actions. It will always lead to truth.

Show love, honesty, integrity, truth and faithfulness to people and they will be your friend.

The young men find glory in their strength, but the old man's glory is in his use of wisdom and common sense.

Punishment is given to cause you to turn away from the wrong you have done. It searches the secrets of your heart.

You may feel you know the right way, but remember, God looks at your motives.

When you do what is proper, honest, right and fair, your actions are pleasing to God. It makes Him happy.

Do not be friends or spend time with those you know are doing evil, wicked things. This pride and lusting after women is sin.

Your actions speak louder than your words. An evil person leads an evil life, but the way or actions of a good person are pure and right.

Help the poor out of what you have. Listen to their cry for help. If you do not care for them, one day you could be like them and no one will help you.

Justice brings joy to the person who follows God. But to the one who does evil, it brings fear.

The young man who pays no attention to common sense will end up as good as dead.

If you desire and practice righteousness, mercy and kindness, you will find righteousness and honor with God.

Guard your conversation; use wisdom and common sense, and you will stay out of trouble.

Be sure of this; Nothing you can think of, including all your own wisdom, knowledge or understanding, can stand against God.

To fear and respect the Lord is the first seed of wisdom. Feed it, let it grow, and it will bring honor, respect and long life for you.

Learn to give and share with the poor and you will be blessed.

If you lead others into sin, your life will end a disaster.

A young man who desires purity and a clean heart will end up being a friend of those in authority

The Lord gives knowledge to the faithful, but the foolish person will be destroyed

A young man's heart is filled with foolishness, but God's discipline, His Word, will remove it.

SPECIAL SAYINGS

L isten closely to what I have to say in the next few words; make these words a part of your life. You will find it good to speak them out loud and often. they will help you keep your trust in the Lord. And continue to seek wisdom and use common sense. These things I tell you now will give you wisdom, understanding and knowledge for your life. You will know the words are the way of truth and will be able to share them with others.

Do not mistrust or abuse the poor and afflicted, just because they are weak and defenseless.

Stay away from an angry and short-tempered person or you will begin acting like them.

Learn the boundaries of life. Respect another person and his ways, and you will have trust and respect from other people.

Work hard, be diligent and skillful in what you do and you will have respect from those in authority over you.

When someone invites you to dinner, watch what they order. Do not order something more costly or better.

It would be better to order less than they do. Because they will notice you, and could be testing you.

Do not desire the finer or better things in life because they can be deceptive, and not good for you.

Do not associate or have anything to do with an evil or self-centered man. He may offer you what seems like something good, but he is only thinking of himself and trying to bribe you or set you up for his good. An important saying is, "As a man thinks in his heart, so is he."

Do not speak words of wisdom to a self-confident person; they will despise what you offer them.

Listen to instruction and criticism, learn from these; seek wisdom, knowledge and common sense.

When you use wisdom and common sense, the heart of God rejoices. When you speak words of wisdom and common sense, God is thrilled with you.

Don't be jealous of sinners, but be zealous for the Lord. Your future is in the hands of God and you will see your desires fulfilled.

Hear what these words say to you, follow the way of the Lord. Do not associate with drunkards or those who drink liquor.

Truth is valuable. Sacrifice your time to know truth. With truth you will get wisdom, knowledge and understanding.

Give your heart, mind and body to the Lord.

Wisdom and common sense tells you that the person who always has trouble with anger, fighting, arguing and complaining has a problem maybe of drinking or drugs. These have a bite like a snake. It's poison makes a person see strange things, say wrong things that would be embarrassing to them when sober. They do not remember what happened, or what they did while under the control of these.

Do not envy or be jealous of sinful men who spend their time thinking of ways to take advantage of people. Do not spend your time with them; avoid them.

A good life is acquired through wisdom and grows with understanding. Common sense gives you a life full of rich and valuable things that are pleasing to the mind and worth very much.

MORE FAVORITE SAYINGS

Common sense increases your power with people. Have many counselors you can count on for advice.

Being led by wisdom, you will overcome the problems of life.

Work to save those who do not follow the Lord; they are lost and heading to death. Do not turn away from them; you must help them to find their way to the Lord.

To gain knowledge and wisdom is good, like eating honey from the honeycomb. It is sweet to the taste, and like this, wisdom is sweet to the soul of man. It will give you a great future.

A man who is right with God may stumble many times in his life, but he will rise again each time. But the sinful man will not rise from his calamity.

Do not be happy or glad when your enemy or the person who hates you fails.

OTHER IMPORTANT TEACHINGS

Y ou are honored when someone gives you a quick honest reply.

Do not try to get even when someone does you wrong.

Do not be a lazy person or the opportunities of life will pass you by. Like a person asleep, you will only dream of good things but never experience them. It will be as if you were robbed of God's plan for your life.

It is through God's greatness that secrets are hidden, but you, the wise person, will look for the answers to these secrets and reveal them.

When you melt silver, take away the waste and the silver is ready for the silversmith to make something of value. If sin is removed from a leader's life, you will see him do what is right and good.

Do not boast of how good you are to those in authority over you. Don't push yourself forward. Be patient and wait for your leader to recognize you. This patience could keep you from being embarrassed and being sent back to the end of the line or being put down in front of all the other people.

Do not be quick to take someone to court. Instead try to work out an agreement with that person.

Watch what you say. Slander can cause your defeat and will cost you in the end. Do not brag to others about how you reached an agreement.

When advice is given in a good way, it is like a gift formed from gold or silver. It is received by the other person and you both are blessed and encouraged by it.

You show wisdom and common sense when you accept valid criticism.

Think on these words; a faithful person is refreshing like a cool breeze on a hot day.

A person who promises a gift but never gives it is like clouds without rain in the desert.

Use wisdom and patience when presenting your thoughts to those in authority over you. Calm speech can break the strongest opposition.

Do not spend much time in visiting with a neighbor or he will become bored and tired of you.

If you tell lies about someone, it will be like you are hitting them with a club or sharp ax.

Be careful when you put confidence in a person who is unreliable. For it will be like chewing with a toothache, or you will be hurt by them.

Do not put confidence in an unfaithful person during a time of trouble. The pain caused by this is like walking on a broken foot.

Do not take revenge on your enemy. If he is hungry, feed him, if he is thirsty give him water. Your concern will confuse him and God will reward you.

If you hear gossip or backbiting about someone, put a stop to it. Otherwise, someone will always be hurt and it could be you.

Always talk about good things. It is like giving a cold drink of water on a hot day.

Do not compromise the good life you are leading. To compromise your integrity is like wallowing in the mud pits.

To seek glory for yourself is an act of pride. You receive glory from others and they will not give to the proud.

A successful person has self control and is an example to those around him.

To give honor to a foolish person is like calling for snow in the summer.

Do not worry about things said about you; let it be like water on a duck's back.

Do not respond to the acts of a fool or you will become like him.

When you respond to a fool, he will think he is superior to you.

When a person acts conceited and wise, pay him no attention; you would have more hope listening to a fool.

A lazy person stays in bed when there is work to be done.

Do not meddle in problems not your own; to do so is like taking a mad dog by the ears

Gossip and quarrels are like wildfire, but if there is nothing to burn, the fire goes out.

Do not brag about what you will do tomorrow; you have no idea what can happen then.

Always let someone else give you praises and never yourself.

A person may falsely accuse you and it may seem a heavy burden, but remember it is false.

Receiving rebuke is better than approval that is never told.
Are you wandering this way and that way? You need to settle down and take count of yourself and what you are doing.

The joy of an honest friend is like sweet perfume to the soul. Be loyal to your friends when things go wrong. Do not run home to your family; it is better to have loyal friends than an uncaring family.

Be thankful for a good friend, for as steel sharpens steel, so a good friend sharpens your facial expressions.

As a person takes care of a fruit tree so he enjoys the fruit, even so you must show honor and respect to those in authority and you will enjoy the benefits.

As a mirror reflects your face, your heart reflects who you are.

You are tested by the praise you receive like gold and silver in the fire.

Don't waste time on a fool; you will never change his foolishness.

Guilt directs the life of the evil wicked person, but the honest person is bold in his actions.

When there is rebellion and trouble, many have different solutions, but a person of wisdom and common sense will show the right way.

Respect and honor God's law and people will look up to you as a man of wisdom. Hang out with the wrong crowd and you embarrass your family.

If you do not pay attention to God's Word, God will not hear your prayers.

Live according to the Bible and you will receive God's blessing. If you lead others wrong, you will fail God.

When a person is right with God, others will honor and respect him. When dictators are in authority, men will run and hide from them.

Do not try to hide your sins. Confess them to God and he will forgive and show compassionate love.

The person who loves God and does his best to serve and follow Him will be happy and satisfied. But the person who hardens his heart against God will have many problems.

If you live a clean life before God, He will reward you. But if you willfully do things contrary to God's way, you will fail.

When you work and are not lazy, you will succeed. But if you are lazy, you will fail.

A man who is faithful in all things will find favor and be blessed. He that develops get rich schemes will end up a failure.

Be careful to show favor to a person; some will sell their soul for a penny.

If you criticize a true friend, rather than agree with him when he is wrong, he will realize and appreciate you.

A proud person causes trouble, but when you live with wisdom and common sense, things will go well with you.

If you think you know it all, you will fail. Learn wisdom and common sense from others.

Give to the poor and be blessed. Turn your back on them and speak harshly of them and you could end up like them.

Be careful to follow discipline. Do not harden to it or you will end up a failure.

Be a good and honest leader and many will follow you. But if you exploit the people, they will fail you.

Live a good life before God and man and you will be happy. But any person is trapped by his own wrong doing.

When you are right with God, you will be concerned about the poor. But the average person will not understand you.

In a disagreement the wise person will control himself, but a foolish person will get angry.

Be thankful for discipline and strong correction. A person left to himself brings disgrace to his family.

Pay close attention to God's leading. Use wisdom and common sense to guide your life, and you will be blessed.

Do not talk before you think or you may have to eat your words.

Be a humble man and not proud, and you will receive honor.

Learn and commit wisdom to your mind. The Creator has made all things and is ultimate wisdom.

God's Word and wisdom are true, search for them. Do not misquote it to serve your own purpose or you will pay dearly.

A YOUNG MAN AND HIS FAMILY

———⟨∞⟩———

Listen to your father and mother; they will give you good instruction. Then live according to their advice. Hide their words in your mind; keep them in your heart, which is the center of life.

This good counsel will lead you to do right all day and all night. It will lead you in your daily walk. You will wake up in the morning thinking about these words.

A wise man will make his father proud of him. But a foolish son will make his mother sad.

Do not provoke you family and loved ones to anger or resentment.. You will only lose them and their love and then what will you have left?

It is good to listen to your father, both to his encouragement and his rebuke.

If your father loves you, he will discipline you. Even so when you have a son, love him but be willing to discipline him.

To Reverence God builds faith and trust. A child finds security in his father's faith.

A foolish young man will despise his father's advice. A son who is wise listens.

A son who speaks ill of his parents, the very ones who gave him life, is a disgrace.

A godly person lives a life of integrity; his family is blessed.

Stay away from the person who speaks bad about his father or mother.

Watch for the special gifts of your children; help them develop these. Train them in the right way and when they get older, they will not depart from this teaching

Discipline your children, correct them when they are wrong. Physical discipline may be required, but this will teach them and in the end they will thank you.

Hear and consider what your father tells you, and when your parents grow old, they will teach you wisdom. Pay attention to what they say.

When you are right and walk in God's ways, your father will be happy and say he has a wise son.

Be wise and bring joy to your father's heart, so he can use you as an example.

When a person steals from his parents and says it is all right, he is an evil person.

Correct and give discipline to your children with love and they will bring joy to your home.

If you pamper your children and let them live without discipline, they will grow up and give you grief and hardship.

A YOUNG MAN AND HIS FINANCES

If you owe someone a debt, pay it as soon as possible. Sacrifice if necessary, don't put it off.

Don't envy people who seem to have everything.

If you have been foolish and your pride will not let you say NO to endorsing a note for someone or making promise to be security for his debt, you face serious problems. You have been trapped by words of your own mouth. Go, swallow your pride. Beg, plead to have your name removed, do it now!

It is best to know a person well before you sign for his credit or bills. It is better to refuse at first than to suffer later by having to pay his bills.

Watch the ants and learn. They don't have a head ruler or leader. They work hard all summer when the weather is good, so they will have food to eat in the winter. But the lazy person wants to sleep. He says, "Let me sleep a little longer, just a little more." The time will come when he cannot work, and the lazy person lives in poverty.

You have heard it said, "Make hay while the sun shines." A farmer works from dawn to dusk when it is time to gather the hay for winter's use. A fool sleeps during this time and loses his crop and soon becomes impoverished and poor.

Like smoke in the eyes and vinegar to the teeth is the lazy person to the one who has hired him.

Love and fear of God will add days to your life. This will give you joy, peace and happiness.

Here is a word of wisdom. When we give to those who are needy, we become richer. The person who is liberal with what he has will become rich. When you share with others, you will grow with God's grace and His law of sowing and reaping comes into effect.

The person who puts his trust in money will lose, but the one who puts his trust in God will grow and be prosperous.

A young man who is willing to work and get his hands dirty at hard work will be prosperous. Hard work returns many blessings.

If you work hard, you will become a leader; be lazy and you will not succeed.

You will be known by your truthfulness, because truth will stand the test of time.

The lazy person always wants more, but has little, while the one who pays attention to his plan and is a hard worker will prosper.

It is better to have little in life along with respect and honor to God, than have much and all the problems that come with disrespect for God.

The man who is dishonest or gets things by doing wrong, brings trouble to his family

Wisdom says, commit your plans to the Lord and your plans will work out well.

A poor man who is honest is better than a man who has gotten wealth in a dishonest way.

Seek God's direction when making plans for your life.

God set the principles of honesty and fairness in every business deal.

Seek wisdom, for it is better to be wise that to have much gold. And wisdom gives understanding which is better than silver.

You may toss a coin to make a choice, but ultimately God controls decisions.

Gold is tested in the furnace, silver in a melting pot, but God tests and purifies the heart of a godly person.

A man does not use wisdom or common sense who co-signs a contract and becomes responsible for the other man's debt.

To make a decision before you know the facts is stupid and will being you shame.

It is better to be a poor man who lives a life of integrity, honesty and truthfulness than to be wealthy and live a false life.

To hurry into something you know nothing about is dangerous and could lead to a sinful life, rebelling against God.

If you are not willing to plow your fields when it is winter or cold, you will have no food at harvest

Work while it is day, for night will come when you cannot work.

A man's plan for life is like a deep well, but a man of wisdom and understanding will draw it out.

Do not love sleep. Rise early, work hard, and you will know a life with plenty.

Be careful when a person buying from you says, "That is worthless". They will go away saying, "Look at the bargain I got."

Listen to common sense and wisdom; they are more valuable than anything money can buy.

You will take a great risk if you make a loan to a stranger. If someone guarantees your loan to a stranger, be sure to get collateral or a deposit.

Any gain you get by cheating may feel good at the time, but later it will feel like gravel or sand in your mouth.

Be sure to seek wisdom before you go ahead with your plans.

If you tell your secrets to a person who talks too much, you can be sure your secret will be told to many people.

To obtain quick wealth, like the lottery, will not be a blessing in the end.

Plan your time, work hard, do your best in everything and you will prosper. Do not try to take short cuts or you could come up short.

Getting wealth by lying or misrepresenting what you have to offer will only lead to poverty or jail.

Those who are dishonest and unfair, do wrong and they will lose in the long run.

To seek fun and pleasure is not the way to go; you will become poor.

The wise young man will save part of all he earns and in the future he will have wealth. But the foolish person will always live from day to day and be poor.

It is better to have a good name and be well thought of than to have great wealth. Favor with your peers is better than much silver and gold.

The rich and poor will stand before God the same. They will not be judged according to wealth or poverty.

Remember this, when you borrow from someone, you become a servant to the lender.

Refuse to sign on a note for someone because they may not pay the debt and you could lose what you have made in payment.

You have heard it said, "First things first." Have a plan for your work, work that plan, then buy or build what you need.

Maintain your finances well; do not make fast money investments. Instead, look over your investments well and they will provide for you.

To be poor but honest is better that to be rich and evil.

Do not plan to get wealth by charging high interest rates. Those who succeed you will be more charitable to the poor.

The person who has gained much wealth thinks he knows everything. But the poor who search for understanding can see right through them.

A WARNING ABOUT GIRLS
AND WOMEN

A pretty girl may approach you in what will seem like innocence. But wisdom will tell you to watch the way she dresses; is it revealing?

It may be acceptable for the day you live in, but does she dress to show parts of her body to entice you? If so, avoid her; she has abandoned all decency and she will use flattery and her body to persuade you to follow her.

Her ways and her bed will lead you to death and hell. Her mind and her body are full of disease. Do what she wants and you will be doomed. You will never be the same after she seduces you.

Instead follow wisdom and common sense. It will lead you the right way and you will enjoy the good life to the full.

Follow the wrong way and you will lose all the good things you might have and you will be destroyed.

Turn away from the easy kiss of a loose girl or prostitute. Keep careful guard over your thought life. Put false teaching away from you, also conversation you know is not good. Walk the walk of truth, taught by wisdom and common sense.

Listen to wisdom. The lips of a strange woman, or prostitute is as sweet as honey and full of flattery. You are not her first victim; she has practiced on many men. She is a smooth talker and knows the right words to entice you. But if you listen to her and give into her, afterwards your conscience will burn with guilt. She will lead you to a path of death and hell.

Wisdom tells you to run from this kind of woman. Don't even go near her, because you might fall for her temptation. She is cruel and merciless and you could end up gnawing in pain and sorrow, when sexually transmitted disease consumes your strength and body.

If you have sex outside of marriage, you are a fool. You destroy yourself and you will live with shame.

Can you carry fire in your hand and not be burned?

Wisdom and common sense will keep you from a girl or woman who is sinful. Guard your thoughts, do not look upon her beauty with lust in your heart. Don't let her smooth words seduce you. If you lie down with a loose girl or woman, your sexual sins could cause you to end up with sexually transmitted diseases that could take your life. Or take you to hell.

Don't let evil or sexual desires get control of you. Don't let your mind dwell on these things. When you follow sinful ways with wrong thoughts, such as pornography, you will end up being destroyed.

Evil people and evil ways are an abomination to God, whose curse is on the wicked. Fools end up in shame but the wise receive honor.

To go one's own way and not seek wisdom or common sense is like a man who listens to a prostitute and follows after her. She says, "come to me, things like this, done in secret, give joy. Stolen melons are best and stolen apples are sweetest." You will end up with all her previous followers, a horrible life in a death bed and in hell.

The wise person recognizes sin and turns away from it. The unwise goes on blindly and suffers for it.

Be aware of the loose woman or prostitute. Her words and actions are like a great trap. The young man who turns his back on God will be caught in this trap and suffer for it. Her diseases will bring long, miserable torment.

There is no love or comfort with a prostitute or loose girls. They take a bath and say, "Who is next?"

Don't waste your virginity on fortune-hunting or promiscuous women or girls. They ruin the lives of many potential great men.

THE YOUNG LADY YOU WILL WANT TO LIVE WITH

⸻᠁⸻

Keep your thoughts pure. Love is good. God planned it, but keep watch on your affections and emotions. They will have influence on all that you do in life.

Be faithful to your wife or wife to be. Let your manhood be a special blessing to your wife and no other. Sex is good and beautiful, full of joy and great pleasure. It was planned by God. So be filled with great joy because you have saved your love for her alone.

Follow the advice of wisdom and common sense. Listen to the words of wisdom. Write them down and read them often.

A life of faithfulness to God will keep you from sin. Follow Bible teaching and you will be safe from sin.

When a man finds a wife who is faithful and loves him, he finds a good thing. She will be a lifelong blessing to him.

Loyalty, kindness, integrity and honesty are what people look for in a person they want to spend their life with.

Remember, what you want or expect of the one to be your wife; she has the right to expect the same from you.

THE WIFE TO BE DESIRED

S he will be morally strong in everything she does. A woman who is strong morally and mentally is a rare person.

The heart of her husband will have confidence and trust in her. And she will attempt to do good for him. She will show what a faithful wife is. You will need to trust her without doubt. She will always be open and honest with you.

A good wife will be laborious and a hard worker. She is not lazy.

She will rise up early before her household and have a good and healthy breakfast ready for her family. And she will prepare for the other meals of the day.

She realizes her worth as a wife and does not stop from her duties early in the day.

She is very wise when it comes to homemaking and the way to direct a household. She has learned the skill of being a wife, taking care of her family. There is no job too big for her and she will always find something to do for her husband.

When it comes to finances, she is careful the way she spends and invests the household money. She looks for the best and good quality bargains and buys them.

She is merciful to the poor and ready to do what she can for them, always ready to help others at a moment's notice with no thought of herself.

She sees to the clothing of her family and they are presented well.

She dresses with strength of purpose and dignity and is not an embarrassment to her husband. She is refined in her taste of clothing.

When she speaks, her words are wise and kindness is the rule when she gives instruction. She uses wisdom and common sense

She will be honored by her family; her children can do nothing but shower praises on her. Her husband will be blessed by her life.

Beauty may soon pass and pleasing people can mislead them, but the woman who loves, serves and worships God, will be admired above all others.

Her husband will say, "There are many good women who have done well and are called great women. But you exceed all of them in virtue and wisdom. You are the best of them all."

This woman deserves the best. Should you find her and she finds you, treat her like a queen.

Other books by Ray Wilson

Tales of My Life

Smoke Signals from God

The Trail to Talking Rock – a parable

Worship the Lord – sent free when you request

15 children's books – first five complete, others due fall 2007

Another one due soon: "Little Owl Learns Wisdom"

To order any of these books or to inquire about them, write to:

Black Buffalo Media
1557 Carlotta Dr.
Hemet, Ca. 92543

Printed in the United States
201868BV00001B/1-414/A